The Elves and
the Shoemaker

Written by Meg Stein
Illustrated by Peter Paul Bajer

sundance

Once upon a time, there was a poor
shoemaker and his wife.
They worked very hard making shoes.
One day, they had just one piece
of shoe leather left.

That night, they cut out the leather
to make their last pair of shoes.
They were very tired. They left the leather
on the bench and went to bed.

In the morning, they found a pair
of new shoes on the bench.
"This is wonderful," said the shoemaker.
"Who made these beautiful shoes?"
asked his wife.

4

A man and a woman came into the shop.
"May I look at those beautiful shoes?"
asked the man. He tried on the shoes.
"These are wonderful shoes," he said.
"I will buy them."

The shoemaker and his wife were happy.
Now they had money to buy
more leather.
That night, they cut out the leather
for two pairs of shoes.

In the morning, they found two pairs
of shoes on the bench.
"This is amazing," said the shoemaker.
"Who made these beautiful shoes?"
asked his wife.

Before long, a man came to the shop
and bought the shoes for his children.

Now the shoemaker had the money
to buy leather for four pairs of shoes.

8

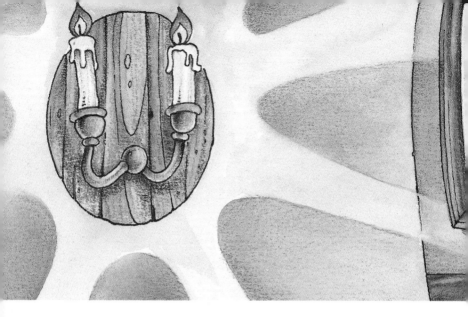

Each night, the same thing happened.
Each morning, there were more shoes.

The shoemaker and his wife had lots
of money, but they still didn't know
who was making the shoes.

One night, they stayed up to see
who was helping them.

They saw two elves come into the shop.
The elves were dressed in rags.
They worked all night
until the shoes were made.

"The elves have been good to us,"
said the wife. "We should make new
clothes and new shoes for them. We will
leave them on the bench tonight."

They worked all day and left the new
clothes and the new shoes on the bench.

When the elves saw the clothes,
they put them on and danced
around the room.

As the sun rose, the two elves danced
through the door and into the street.

The shoemaker and his wife lived happily
ever after.